EASY GUITAR
WITH NOTES & TAB

ADELE

ISBN 978-1-4584-1686-5

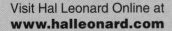

Visit Hal Leonard Online at
www.halleonard.com

HAL•LEONARD®
CORPORATION
7777 W. BLUEMOUND RD. P.O. BOX 13819 MILWAUKEE, WI 53213

STRUM AND PICK PATTERNS

This chart contains the suggested strum and pick patterns that are referred to by number at the beginning of each song in this book. The symbols ⊓ and ∨ in the strum patterns refer to down and up strokes, respectively. The letters in the pick patterns indicate which right-hand fingers play which strings.

p = thumb
i = index finger
m = middle finger
a = ring finger

For example; Pick Pattern 2
is played: thumb - index - middle - ring

Strum Patterns

Pick Patterns

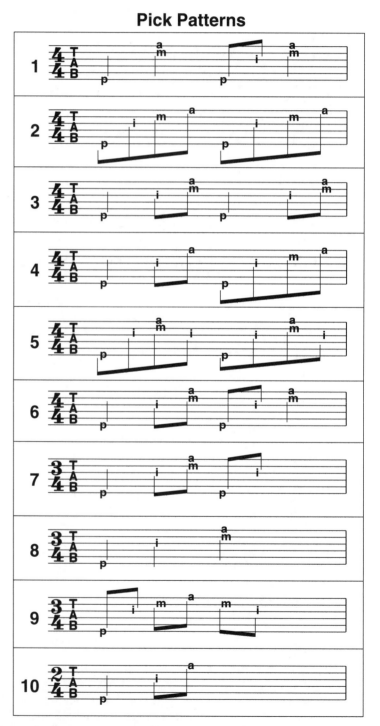

You can use the 3/4 Strum and Pick Patterns in songs written in compound meter (6/8, 9/8, 12/8, etc.). For example, you can accompany a song in 6/8 by playing the 3/4 pattern twice in each measure. The 4/4 Strum and Pick Patterns can be used for songs written in cut time (¢) by doubling the note time values in the patterns. Each pattern would therefore last two measures in cut time.

Chasing Pavements

Words and Music by Adele Adkins and Francis Eg White

*Tune down 1 step:
(low to high) D-G-C-F-A-D

Strum Pattern: 4, 5
Pick Pattern: 4, 5

*Optional: To match recording, tune down 1 step.

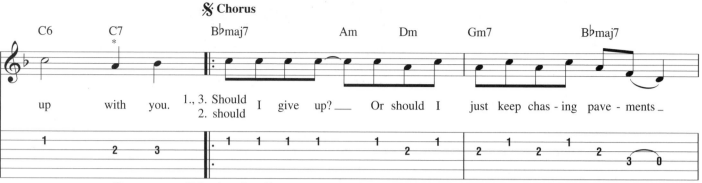

%. **Chorus**

*Sung one octave higher throughout Chorus.

To Coda ⊕

**Sung as written.

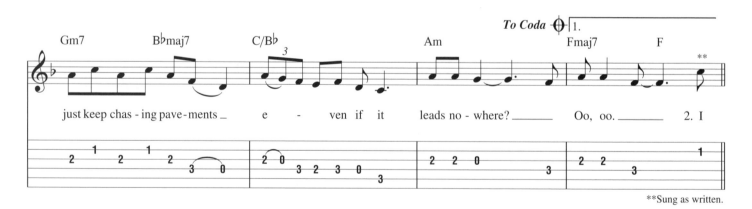

Verse

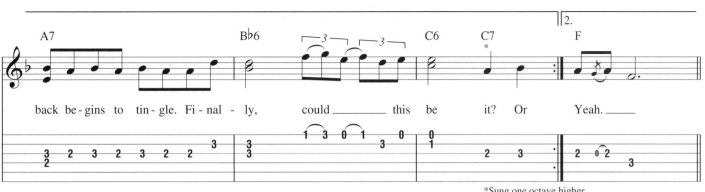

back be-gins to tin-gle. Fi-nal-ly, could _____ this be it? Or Yeah. _____

*Sung one octave higher.

Bridge

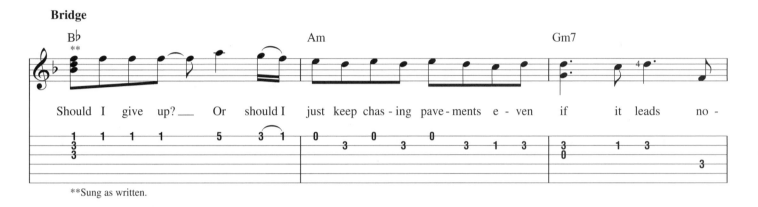

Should I give up? _____ Or should I just keep chas-ing pave-ments e-ven if it leads no-

**Sung as written.

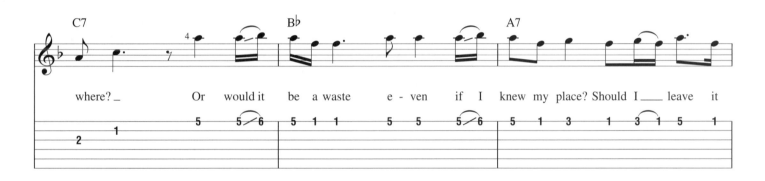

where? _____ Or would it be a waste e-ven if I knew my place? Should I _____ leave it

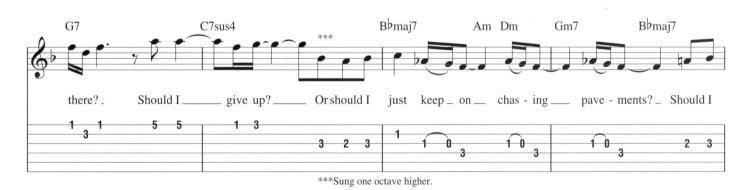

there? _____ Should I _____ give up? _____ Or should I just keep _ on _ chas-ing _____ pave-ments? _ Should I

***Sung one octave higher.

D.S. al Coda Coda

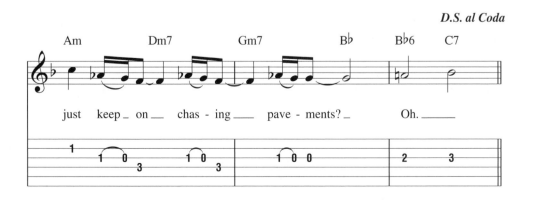
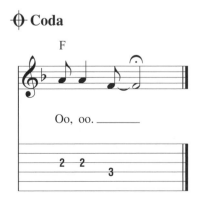

just keep _ on _ chas-ing _____ pave-ments? _ Oh. _____   Oo, oo. _____

Daydreamer

Words and Music by Adele Adkins

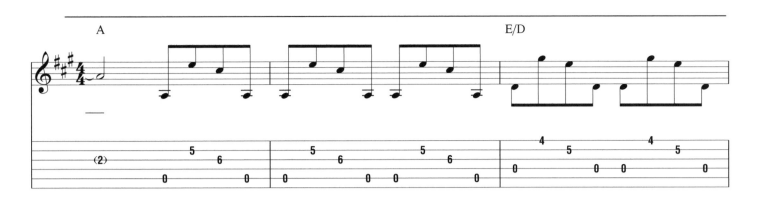

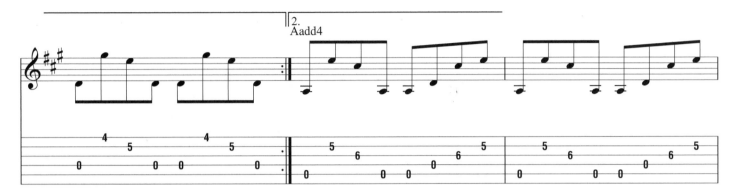

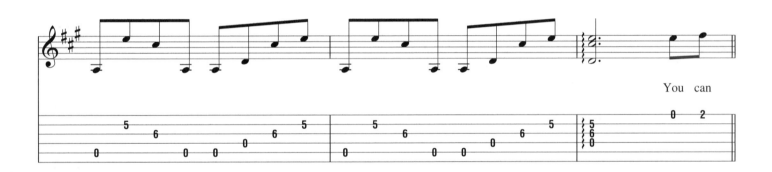

☙ Chorus

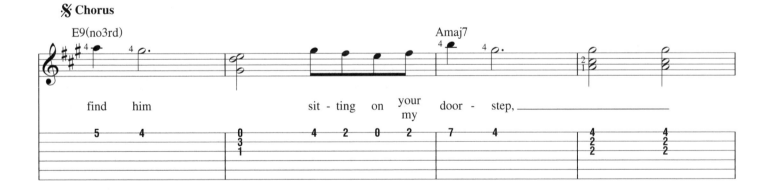

find   him   sit - ting   on   your   door - step,
                                          my

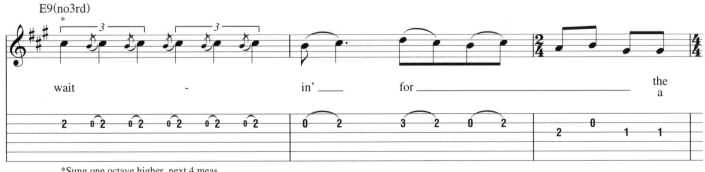

wait - in' ____   for _____   the
                                                  a

*Sung one octave higher, next 4 meas.

sur - prise.   And he will   feel   like   he's been   there   for

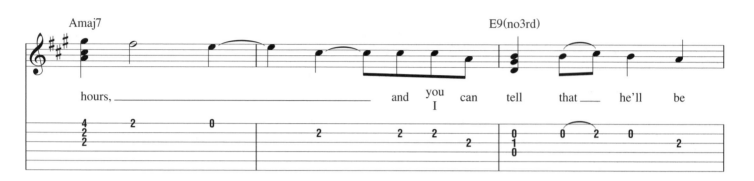

hours, _____ and   you   can   tell   that ___   he'll   be
                                                    I

To Coda 2 ⊕   *D.C. al Coda 1*   ⊕ **Coda 1**

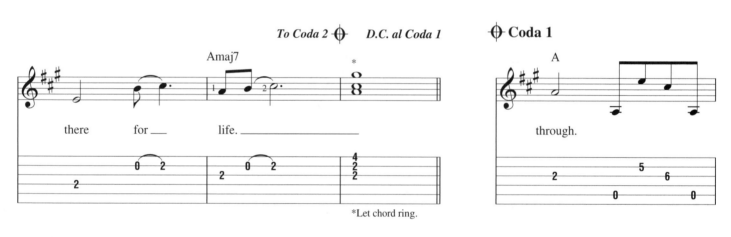

there   for ___   life. _____   through.

*Let chord ring.

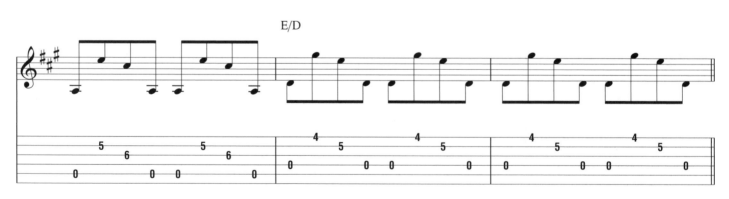

Bridge

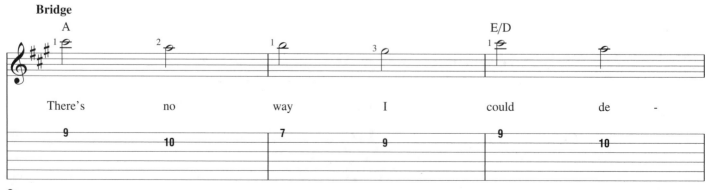

There's   no   way   I   could   de -

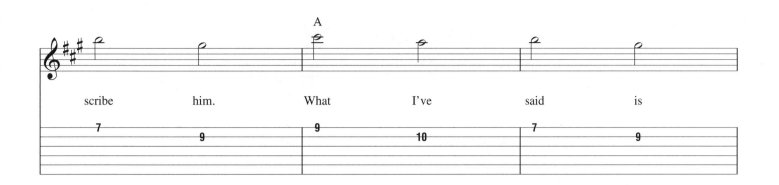

scribe him. What I've said is

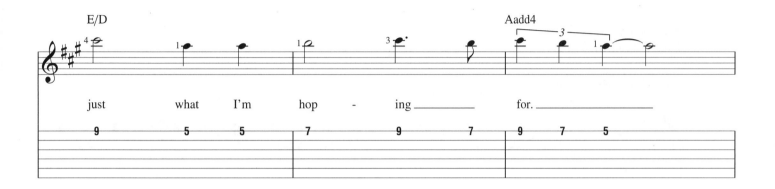

just what I'm hop - ing _____ for. _____

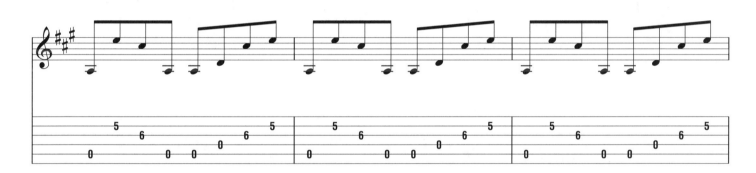

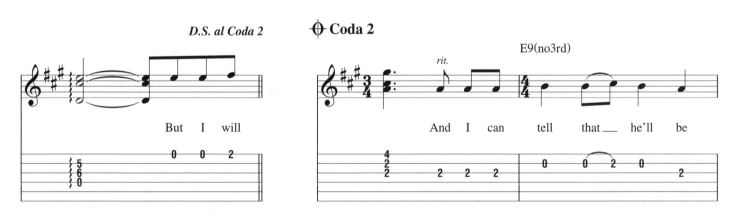

But I will

And I can tell that __ he'll be

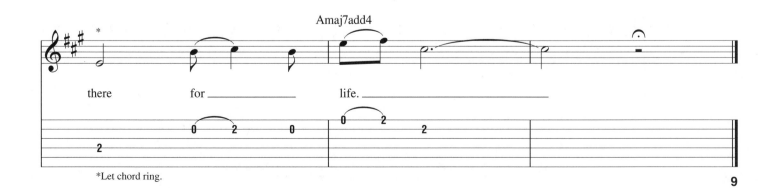

there for _____ life. _____

*Let chord ring.

Lovesong

**Words and Music by Robert Smith, Laurence Tolhurst, Simon Gallup,
Paul S. Thompson, Boris Williams and Roger O'Donnell**

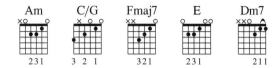

*Capo III

Strum Pattern: 5
Pick Pattern: 4

Intro
Moderately slow, in 2

*Optional: To match recording, place capo at 3rd fret.

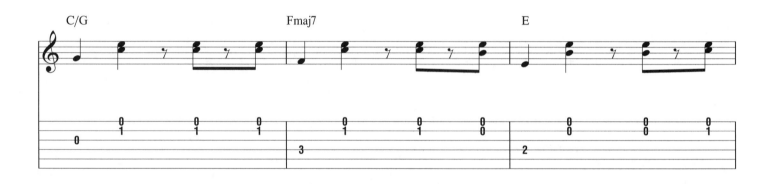

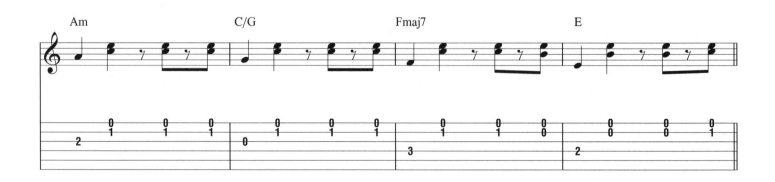

Verse

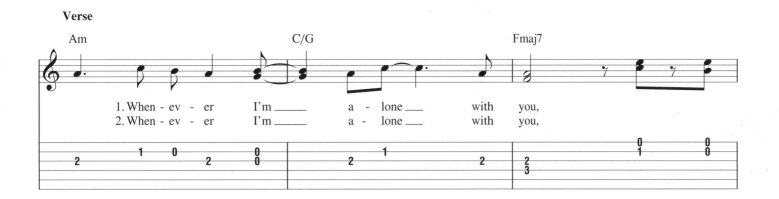

1. When - ev - er I'm _____ a - lone _____ with you,
2. When - ev - er I'm _____ a - lone _____ with you,

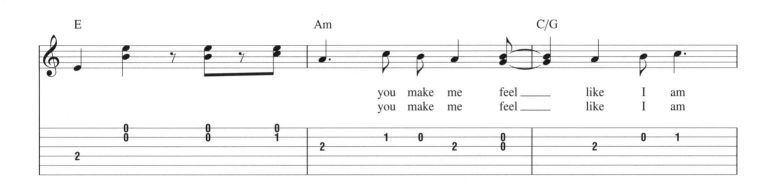

you make me feel _____ like I am
you make me feel _____ like I am

home a - gain. _____
young a - gain. _____

When - ev - er I'm _____
When - ev - er I'm _____

_____ a - lone _____ with you,
_____ a - lone _____ with you,

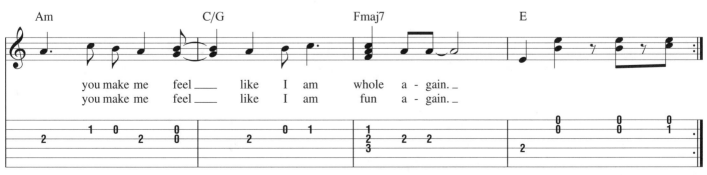

you make me feel _____ like I am whole a - gain. _____
you make me feel _____ like I am fun a - gain. _____

3rd time, To Coda 2 ⊕

However far away, _____ *I will al - ways love_ you.*

However long_ I stay, _____ *I will al - ways love_ you.*

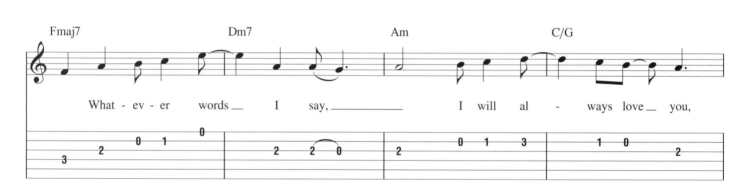

What - ev - er words_ I say, _____ *I will al - ways love_ you,*

To Coda 1 ⊕
Interlude

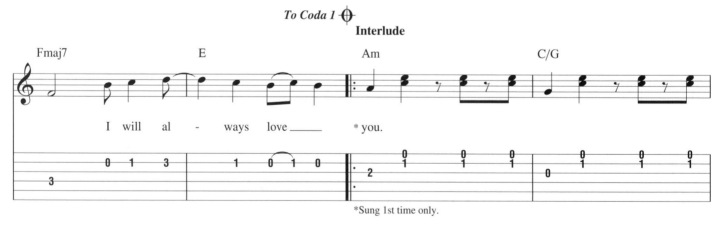

I will al - ways love _____ ** you.*

*Sung 1st time only.

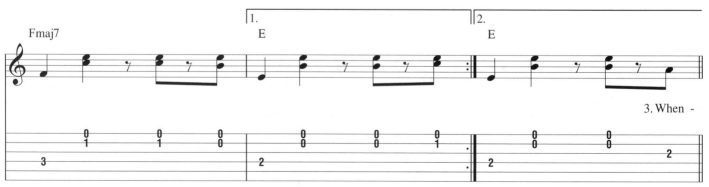

3. When -

Verse

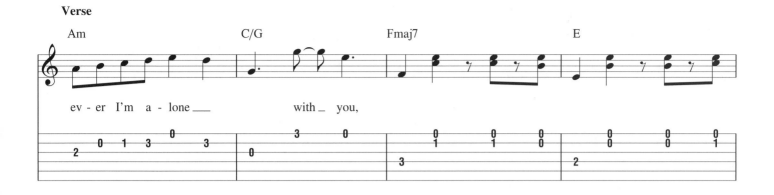

ev - er I'm a - lone ___ with ___ you,

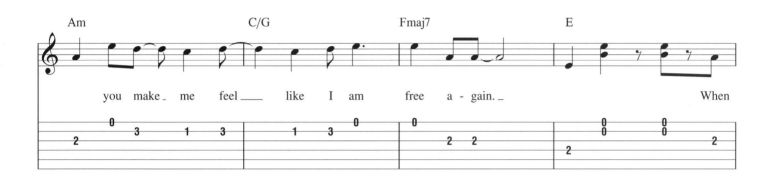

you make ___ me feel ___ like I am free a - gain. ___ When

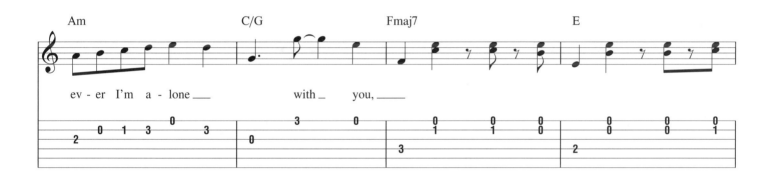

ev - er I'm a - lone ___ with ___ you, ___

D.S. al Coda 1

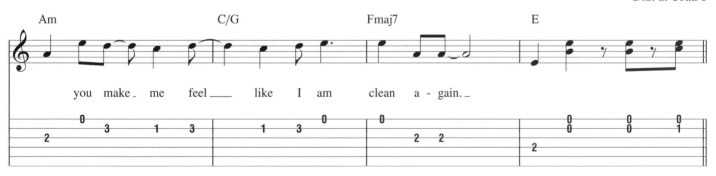

you make ___ me feel ___ like I am clean a - gain. ___

Coda 1

Guitar Solo

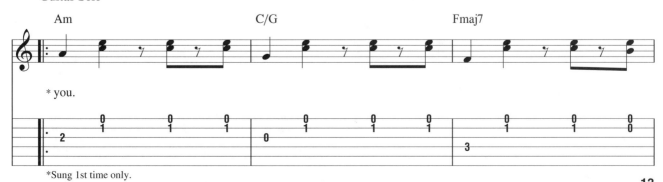

* you.

*Sung 1st time only.

Make You Feel My Love

Words and Music by Bob Dylan

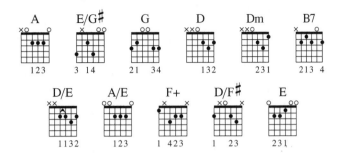

*Capo I

Strum Pattern: 6
Pick Pattern: 6

Intro
Moderately

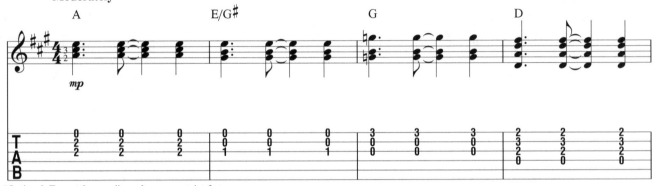

*Optional: To match recording, place capo at 1st fret.

Verse

1. When the rain _ is blow-ing in your face, _ and the whole _ world is
2. When the eve-ning shat-ters and the stars ap - pear, _ and there is no ___ one there to
4. *Instrumental*

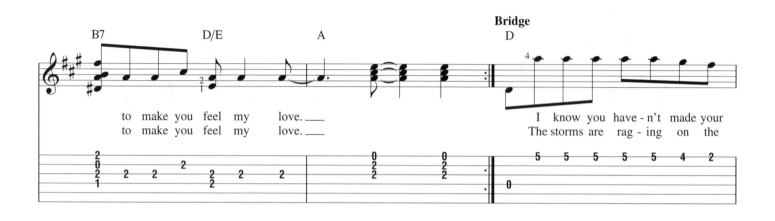

Verse

yet.

3. I'd go hun - gry, I'd go black and blue, ___

5. I could make you hap - py, make your dreams come true, ___

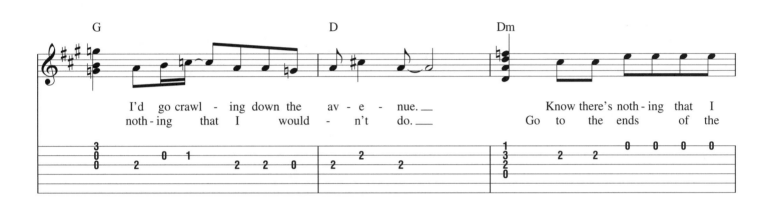

I'd go crawl - ing down the av - e - nue. ___

noth - ing that I would - n't do. ___

Know there's noth - ing that I

Go to the ends of the

To Coda ⊕

D.S. al Coda
(no repeat)

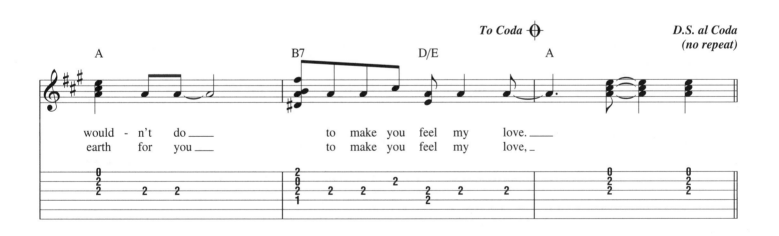

would - n't do ___

earth for you ___

to make you feel my love. ___

to make you feel my love, ___

⊕ **Coda**

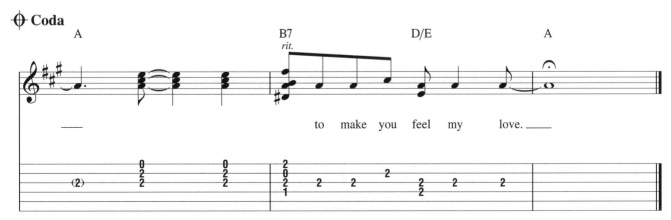

___

to make you feel my love. ___

One and Only

Words and Music by Adele Adkins, Dan Wilson and Greg Wells

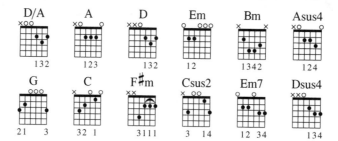

*Capo III

Strum Pattern: 7
Pick Pattern: 8

Intro
Slowly

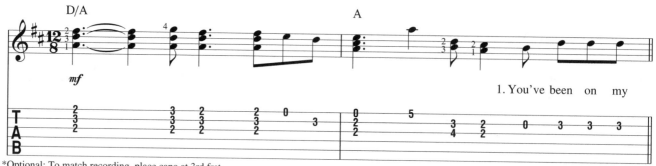

1. You've been on my

*Optional: To match recording, place capo at 3rd fret.

Verse

mind,
mind? I grow fon-der ev-'ry day. Lose my-self in
You hang on ev-'ry word I say, lose your-self in

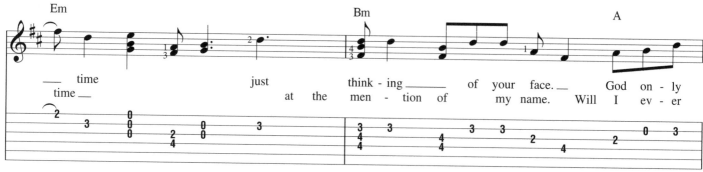

___ time just think-ing ___ of your face. God on-ly
time ___ at the men-tion of my name. Will I ev-er

knows ___ why it's tak-en me so long ___ to let my doubts ___
know ___ how it feels to hold you close ___ and have you

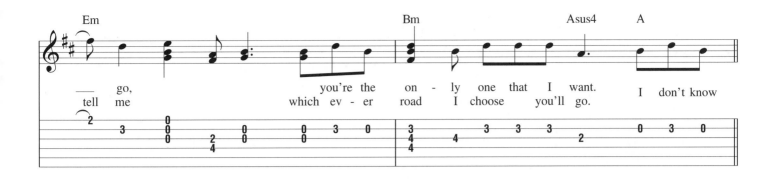

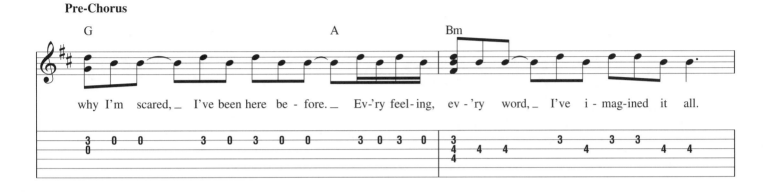

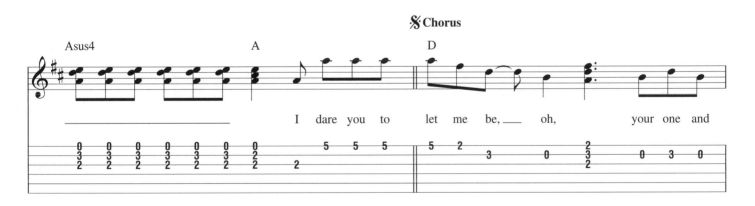

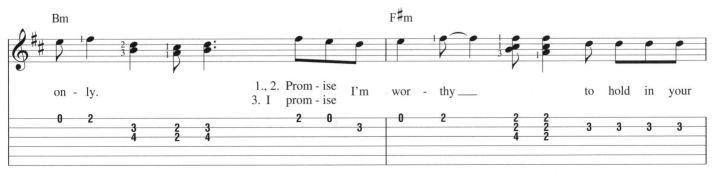

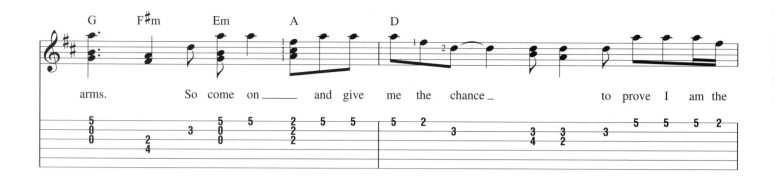

arms.   So come on _____ and give   me   the   chance _   to prove I   am   the

To Coda ⊕

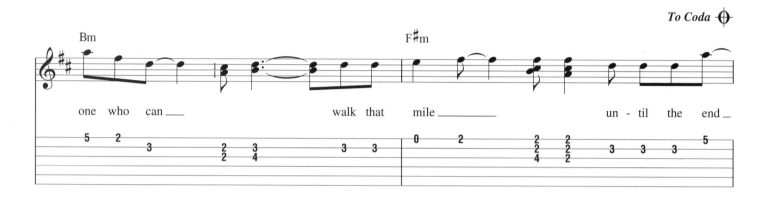

one   who   can _____   walk   that   mile _____   un - til   the   end _

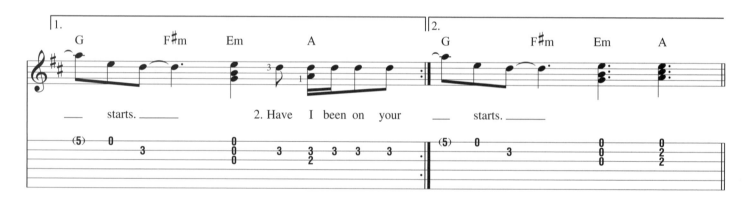

_ starts. _____   2. Have   I   been   on   your   _ starts. _____

Bridge

I know   it ain't eas - y _____   giv-ing up _ your heart.   I know   it ain't eas - y _____

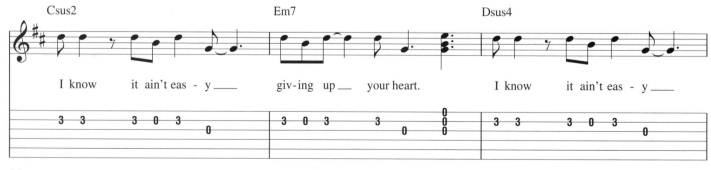

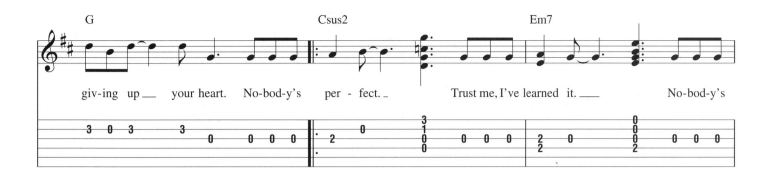

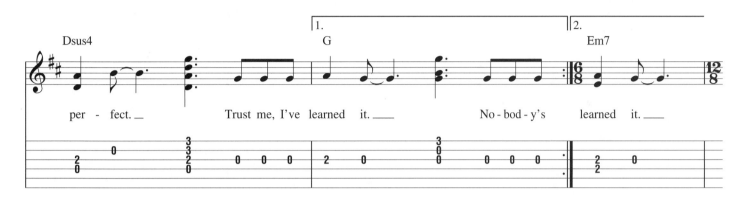

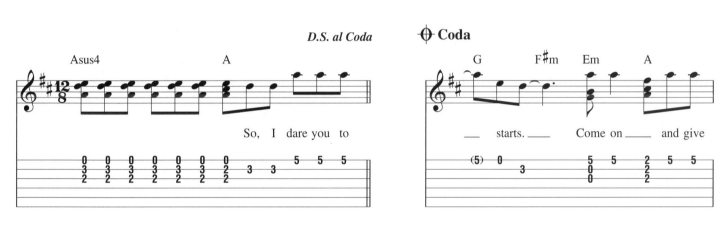

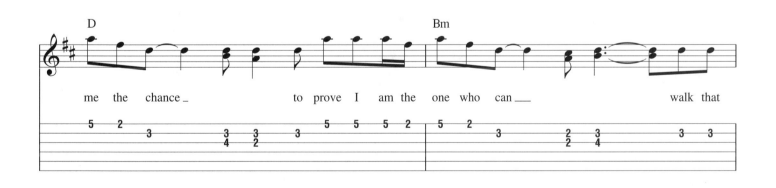

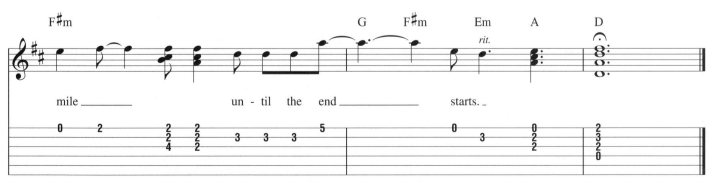

Right as Rain

Words and Music by Adele Adkins, Leon Michels, Jeff Silverman, Clay Holley and Nick Movshon

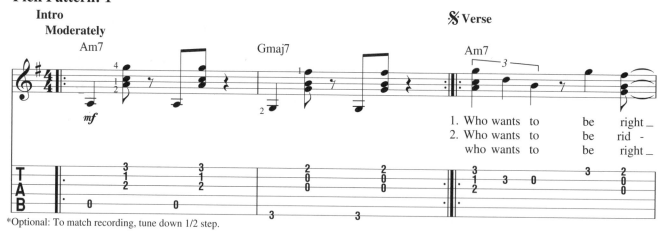

*Tune down 1/2 step:
(low to high) E♭-A♭-D♭-G♭-B♭-E♭

Strum Pattern: 5
Pick Pattern: 1

Intro
Moderately

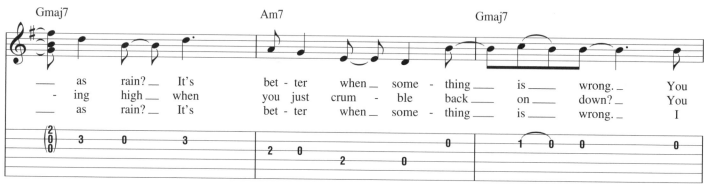

*Optional: To match recording, tune down 1/2 step.

1. Who wants to be right as rain? It's bet-ter when some-thing is wrong. You
2. Who wants to be rid-ing high when you just crum-ble back on down? You
   who wants to be right as rain? It's bet-ter when some-thing is wrong. I

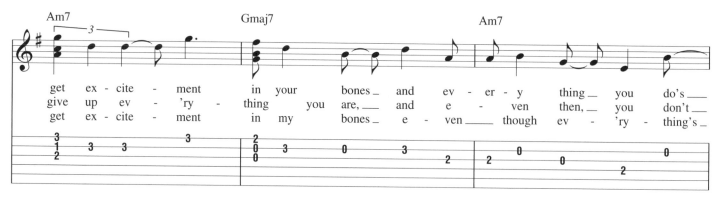

get ex-cite-ment in your bones and ev-er-y thing you do's
give up ev-'ry-thing you are, and e-ven then, you don't
get ex-cite-ment in my bones e-ven though ev-'ry-thing's

a game. When night comes and you're on your own, you can say,
get far. They make be-lieve that ev-'ry-thing is ex-act-
a strain. When night comes and I'm on my own, you should know

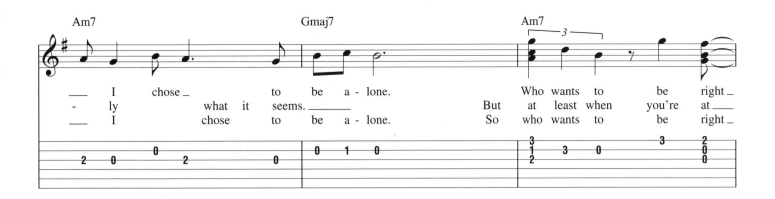

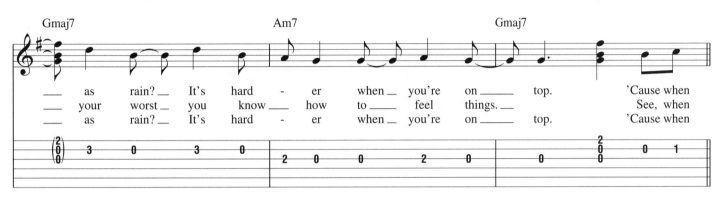

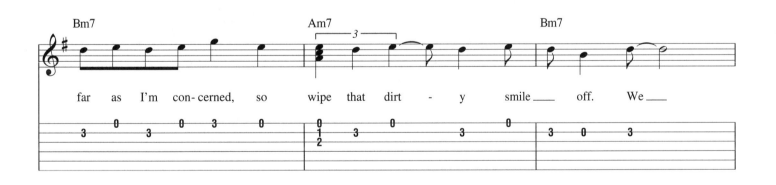

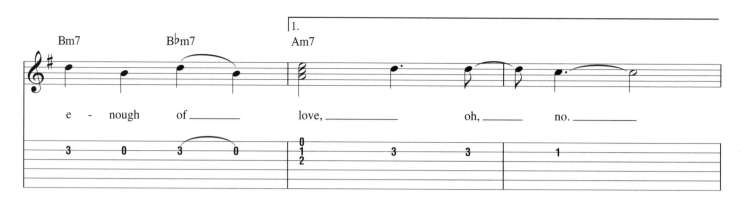

e - nough of _____ love, _____ oh, _____ no. _____

Bridge

love. Go a-head and steal my heart to

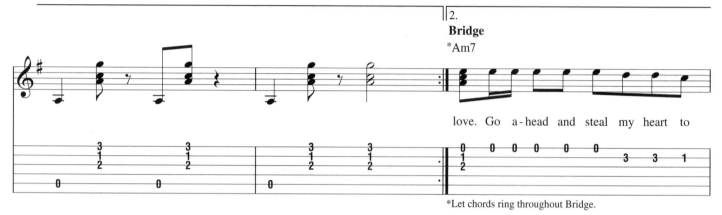

*Let chords ring throughout Bridge.

make me cry a-gain, 'cause it will nev-er hurt as much as it did then, when

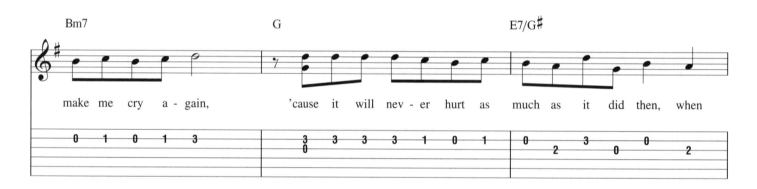

we were both right and no one had blame,_ but now I give up on this

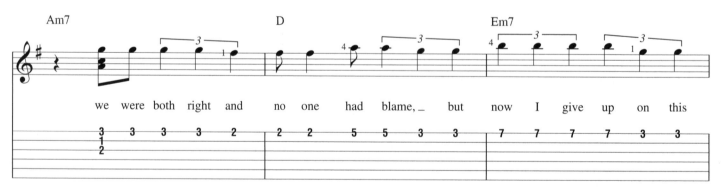

⊕ Coda

D.S. al Coda

Chorus

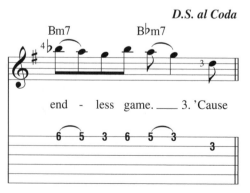

end - less game._ 3. 'Cause

no room in my bed as far as I'm con - cerned, so
No

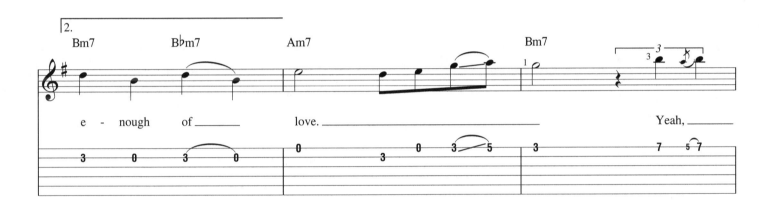

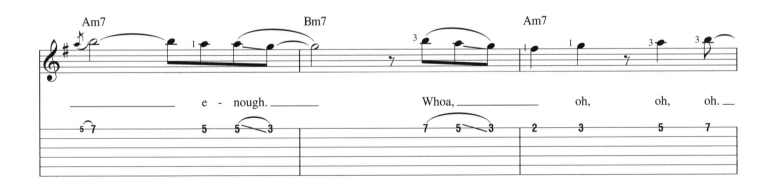

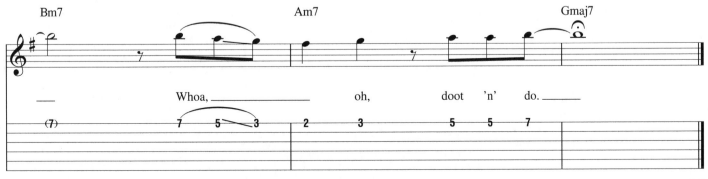

Rolling in the Deep

Words and Music by Adele Adkins and Paul Epworth

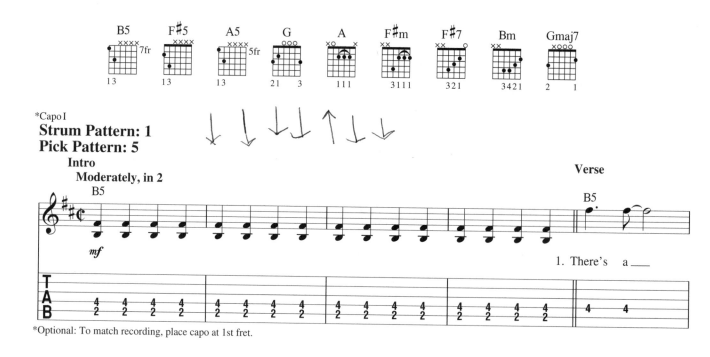

*Capo I

Strum Pattern: 1
Pick Pattern: 5

*Optional: To match recording, place capo at 1st fret.

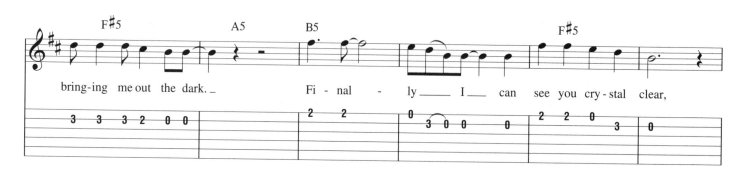

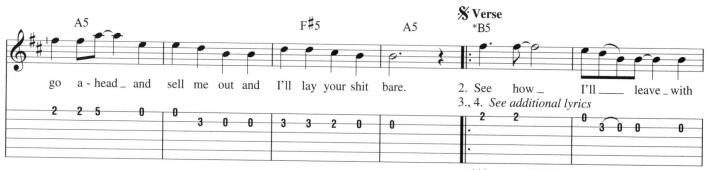

*4th verse, N.C.(Bm), next 16 meas.

*Sung one octave higher, next 8 meas.

had my heart in - side _____ of your hand, ___ and you played __ it to the beat. __

We could have had it all. _____

Roll-ing in the deep. _____ You had my heart in - side _____ of your hand, _____

*Sung one octave higher, next 8 meas.

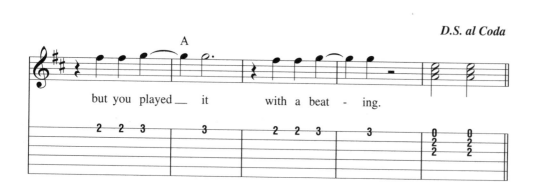

but you played __ it with a beat - ing.

(You're gon-na wish you _

**Notation in Bridge is a composite of background and lead vocals.

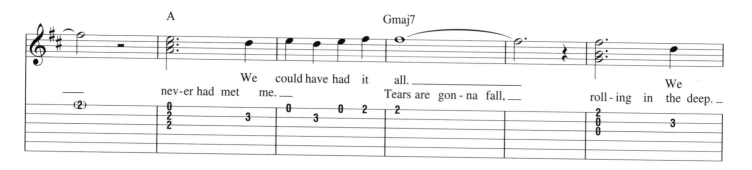

We could have had it all. _____
nev-er had met me. __ Tears are gon - na fall, _ roll-ing in the deep. _

*Sung one octave higher, next 8 meas.

Additional Lyrics

3. Baby, I have no story to be told,
But I've heard one on you,
Now I'm gonna make your head burn.
Think of me in the depths of your despair,
Make a home down there,
As mine sure won't be shared.

4. Throw your soul through every open door,
Count your blessings
To find what you look for.
Turn my sorrows into treasured gold.
You'll pay me back in kind,
And reap just what you've sown.

Rumour Has It

Words and Music by Adele Adkins and Ryan Tedder

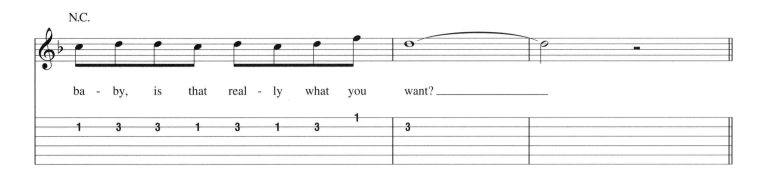

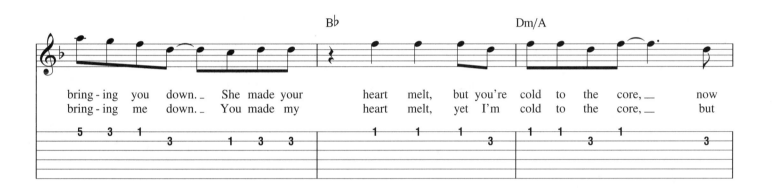

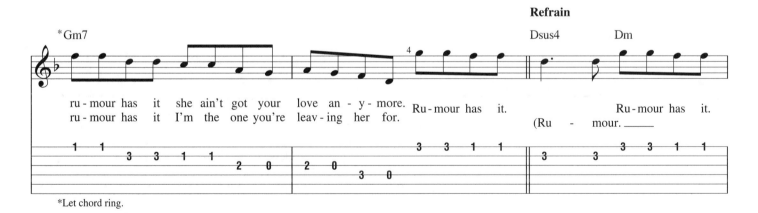

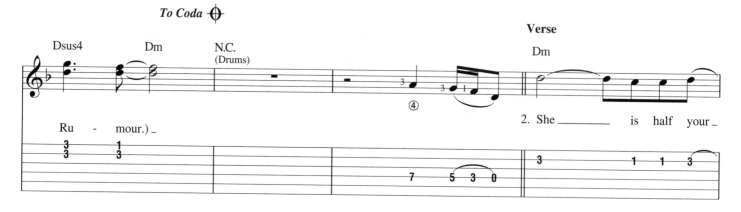

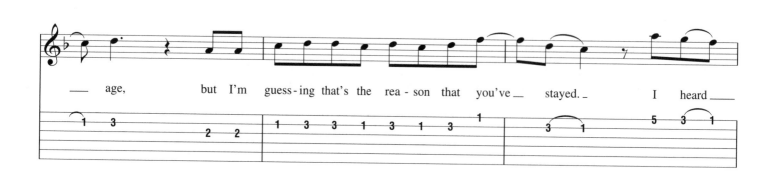

Someone Like You

Words and Music by Adele Adkins and Dan Wilson

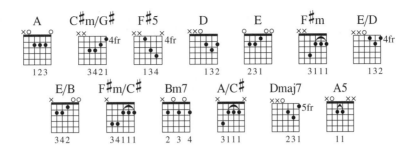

*Strum Pattern: 3
*Pick Pattern: 3

Intro
Slowly

*Use Pattern 10 for   meas.

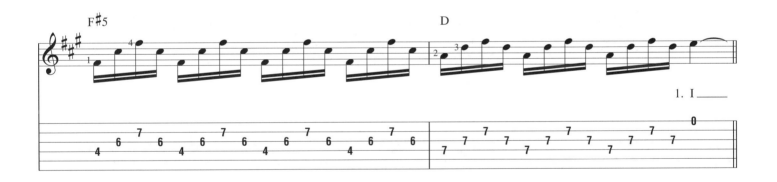

Verse

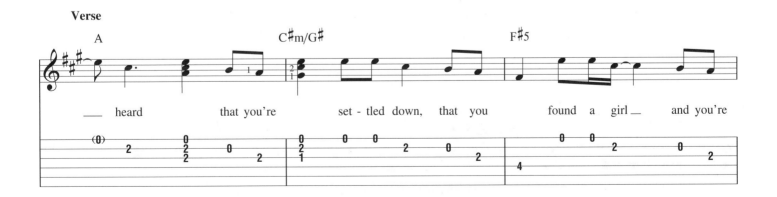

____ heard   that you're   set - tled down,   that you   found a girl ____   and you're

mar - ried now. _____ I heard _ that your dreams came true, guess she

gave you things _____ I did-n't give to you. _____ Old friend, why are you so _

_ shy? _ Ain't like you to hold _ back _ or _ hide _ from the light. _ I

Pre-Chorus

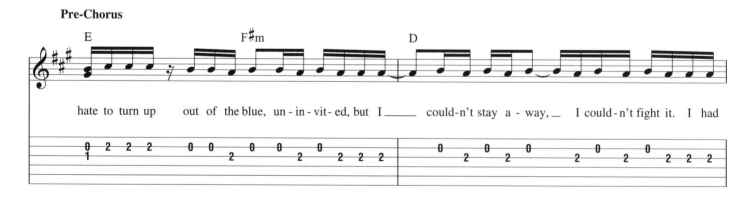

hate to turn up out of the blue, un - in - vit - ed, but I _____ could-n't stay a - way, _ I could-n't fight it. I had

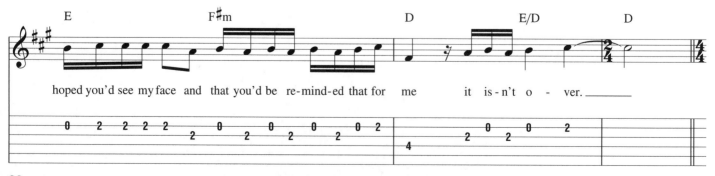

hoped you'd see my face and that you'd be re-mind-ed that for me it is-n't o - ver. _____

*Sung one octave higher.

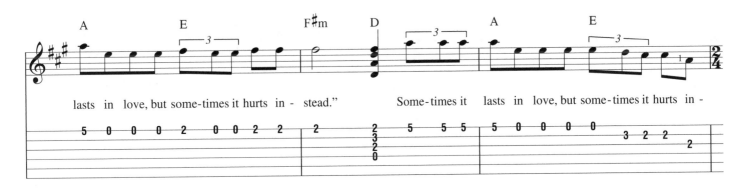

Verse

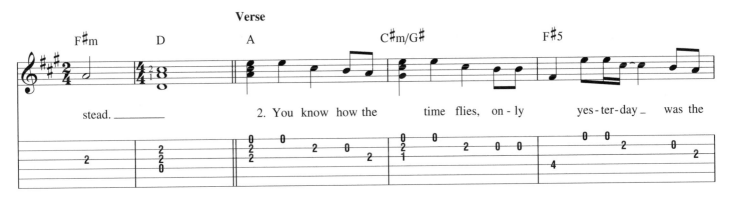

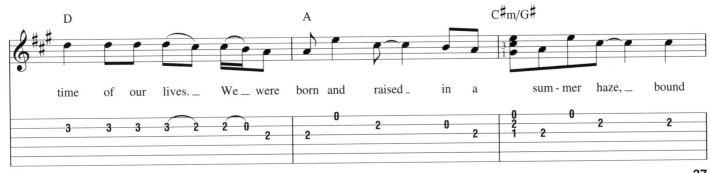

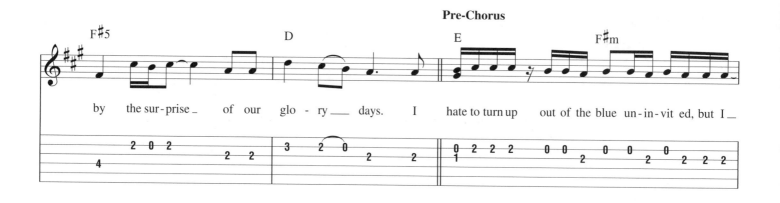

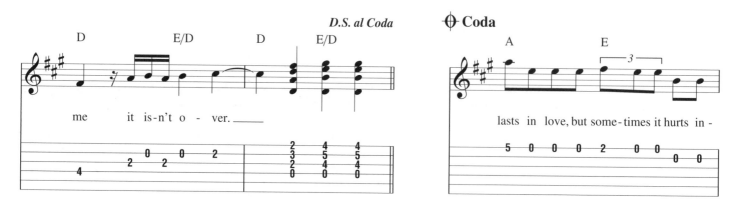

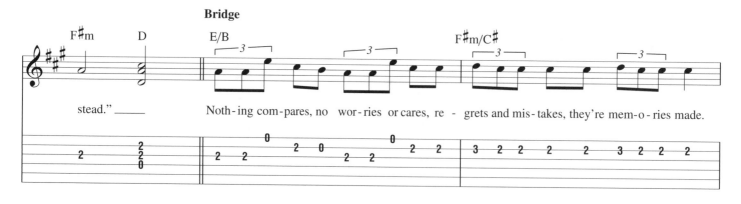

Nev-er - mind,_ I'll find some-one like __ you, _____ I wish noth - ing but the best for

you two. Don't for - get me, I beg, I ___ re - mem-ber you said, ___ "Some-times it

*Sung one octave higher.

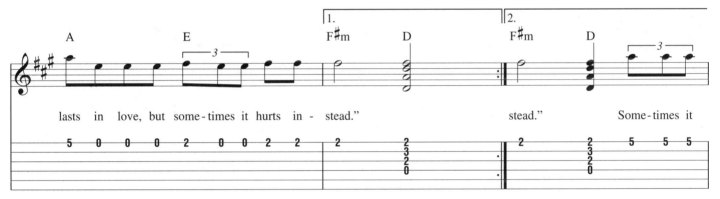

lasts in love, but some-times it hurts in - stead."   stead."   Some-times it

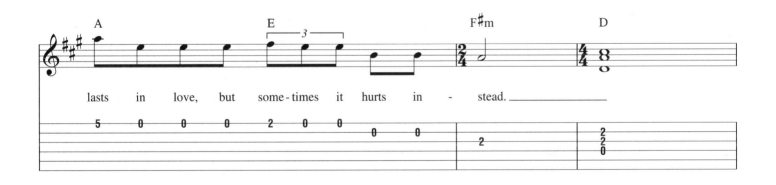

lasts in love, but some-times it hurts in - stead. _____

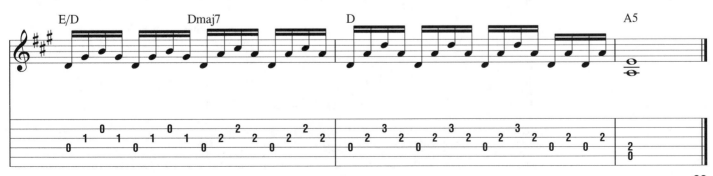

Set Fire to the Rain

Words and Music by Adele Adkins and Fraser Smith

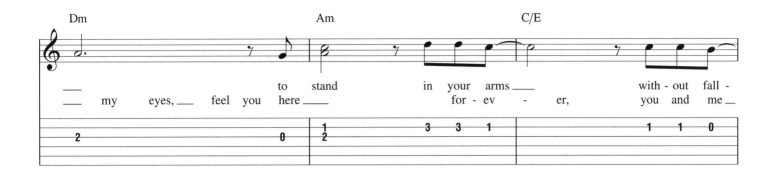

Pre-Chorus

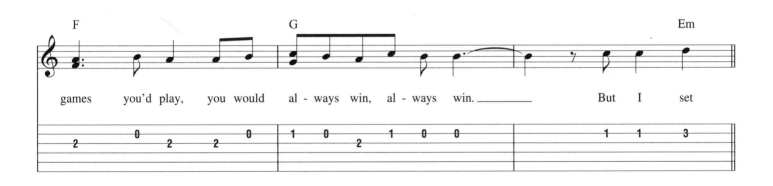

Chorus

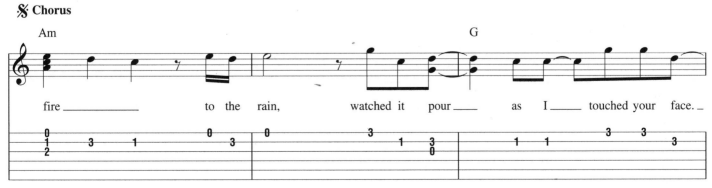

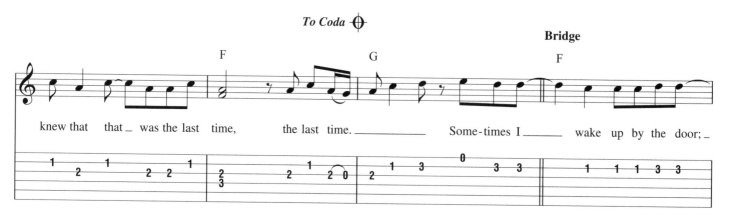

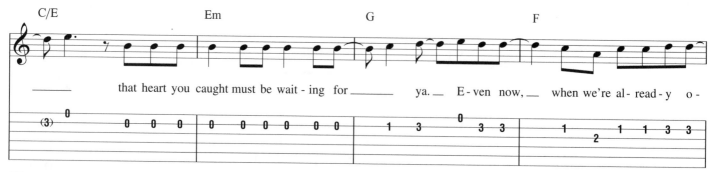

Turning Tables

Words and Music by Adele Adkins and Ryan Tedder

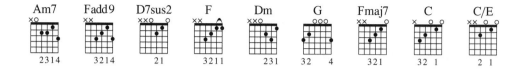

*Capo III

Strum Pattern: 1

Pick Pattern: 5

Intro

Moderately, in 2

*Optional: To match recording, place capo at 3rd fret.

Verse

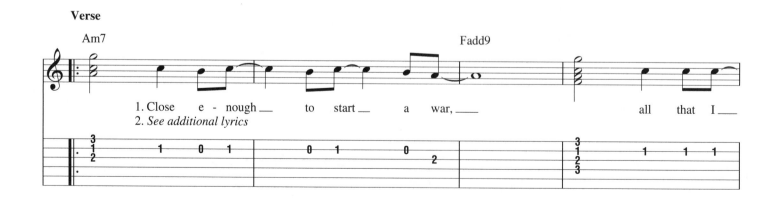

1. Close e-nough ___ to start ___ a war, ___ all that I ___

2. *See additional lyrics*

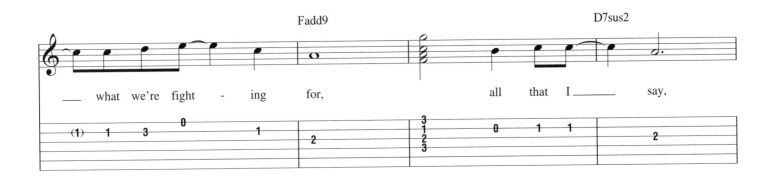

*Let chord ring.

close e-nough_ to hurt___ me, no I _____ won't res - cue

you to just ___ de-sert ___ me. I can't give you the

heart you think_ you gave___ me, _____ it's time to say good-bye_____

*Let chord ring.

To Coda ⊕

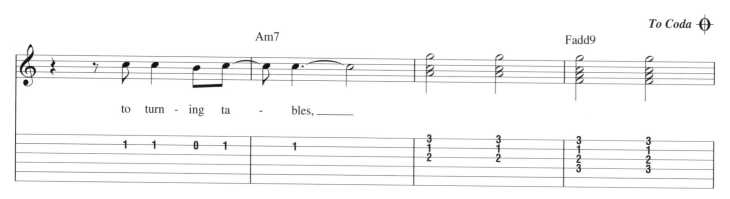

to turn-ing ta - bles, _____

1.

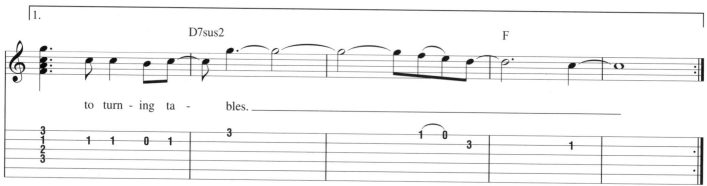

to turn-ing ta - bles. _____

turn - ing ta - bles. _____

Bridge

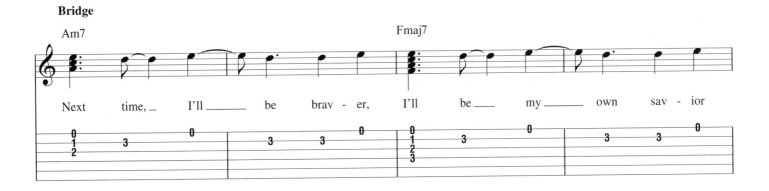

Next time, __ I'll ____ be brav - er, I'll be ___ my ____ own sav - ior

when the thun - der calls __ for me. ____

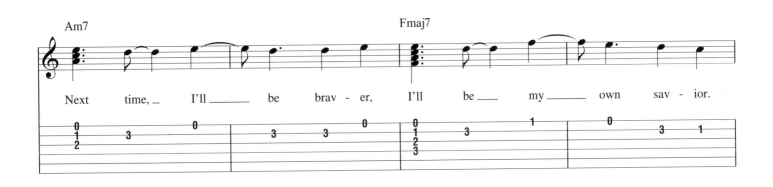

Next time, __ I'll ____ be brav - er, I'll be ___ my ____ own sav - ior.

D.S. al Coda

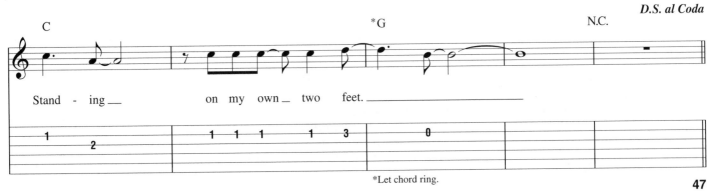

Stand - ing ___ on my own __ two feet. ____

*Let chord ring.

Coda

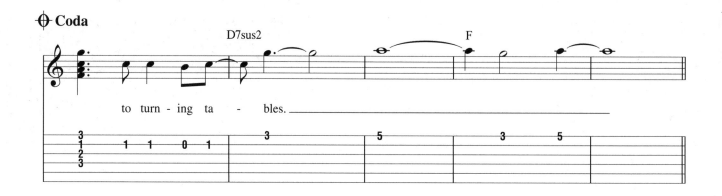

to turn - ing ta - bles. _____

Outro

w/ Lead Voc. ad lib.

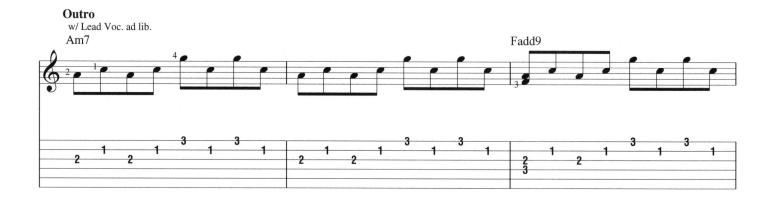

Additional Lyrics

2. Under hardest guise I see, oo,
   Where love is lost, your ghost is found.
   I braved a hundred storms to leave you,
   As hard as you try, no, I will never be knocked down.